Original title:
The Beauty of Tropical Light

Copyright © 2025 Creative Arts Management OÜ
All rights reserved.

Author: Samuel Kensington
ISBN HARDBACK: 978-1-80581-600-3
ISBN PAPERBACK: 978-1-80581-127-5
ISBN EBOOK: 978-1-80581-600-3

Harmony of Light and Lush Growth

In the jungle the sun plays peek-a-boo,
Leaves wearing shades, they think it's cool.
A parrot winks, showing off his flair,
While monkeys dance, without a care.

Coconuts roll like they're in a race,
Palm trees sway, just keeping pace.
Lizards lounge, soaking up the rays,
Trying to tan in their own funny ways.

The flowers giggle, colors so bright,
As butterflies flit in pure delight.
A toucan's beak, like a rainbow's grin,
Makes every day feel like a win.

Even the shadows join in the fun,
Stretching and yawning, they're never done.
Chasing the light like a silly game,
In this lush world, nothing's the same!

A Swirl of Light and Life

Sunlight's dance upon the waves,
Fish wear sunglasses, misbehaves.
Palms do the limbo, sway with glee,
While crabs throw parties, wild and free.

Beach balls bounce in a sunny fight,
Seagulls squawk in pure delight.
Flip-flops fly, a family feud,
As laughter echoes, joy's renewed.

Dawn's Warm Embrace on Island Shores

Morning rises, bright and loud,
Coffee cups held by a sleepy crowd.
Bacon sizzles, birds start to chirp,
Even the waves join in the burp.

Sunbeams tickle sleepy heads,
Sandcastles rise like buttered breads.
The tide whispers secrets, soft and sly,
As laughter spills beneath the sky.

Effulgence of Life's Moments

Hot sun kisses every cheek,
Sunburned noses, oh so chic!
Lemonade spills in sticky pools,
While turtles wear the finest jewels.

Ice cream drips on sandy toes,
Mangoes cheer as laughter flows.
Jellyfish dance in a jelly band,
As children swoop in, cheers so grand.

Chasing Shadows with Rays of Hope

Shadows chase the daytime sun,
Frolicking, just having fun.
Hammocks sway with a happy tune,
While licked ice cream melts too soon.

The sun dips low, like a prankster sly,
Pink skies giggle, oh my, oh my!
Flip-flops flopped on sandy trails,
As night settles, the laughter sails.

Radiant Colors of Nature's Canvas

A parrot in a tutu flies,
The sun spills orange through the skies.
Coconuts giggle as they sway,
Thinking 'Oh, what a bright, fine day!'

Sunscreen fights with sand's embrace,
Flip-flops dance, a wobbly race.
Bananas wear sunglasses bright,
While crabs perform with pure delight.

Celestial Brushstrokes of Dawn

A rooster crows in plaid pajamas,
The sky is full of ripe guanas.
Coffee brews with a cheeky grin,
As tropical winds begin to spin.

Mangoes juggle in the breeze,
While palm trees giggle with such ease.
Waves tease toes in sandy shoes,
And seagulls shout their morning news.

Serene Sunsets Over Palm Fronds

The sun dips low, it's quite a show,
Palm fronds wave, putting on a glow.
A hermit crab in flip-flops found,
Crosses the beach while spinning round.

Light dances on the ocean's face,
While friends compete in a sandcastle race.
A beach ball soars, dodging the rays,
Making memories in silly ways.

Enchanted by Tropical Glow

Fireflies host a limbo night,
As stars flicker, counting their light.
Coconuts laugh at the moon's bright face,
While owls hoot with a hint of grace.

Ice cream cones with faces bright,
Melting quick in the warm delight.
Tropical breezes tease with charm,
As lizards play the night alarm.

Emerald Glow Beneath Tropical Skies

In the jungle, the sun's a joker,
Painting leaves like a gleeful pok-er.
Lizards dance with shades of green,
Tickling vines, they steal the scene.

Coconuts giggle, swaying high,
While crabs conspire with a sly goodbye.
Beneath the palm, shadows play tricks,
As sunbeams burst like playful flicks.

Rays of Joy Amidst Mango Trees

Mangoes hanging like laughter on limbs,
Each one a sunray, overflowing whims.
Squirrels chortle, stealing the show,
While bees do the tango, buzzing below.

Bright rays tickle every ripe fruit,
Encouraging ants to dance with their loot.
They march in lines, a wobbly parade,
In this sweet haven, joy's serenade.

Iridescence of Dawn's Embrace

Morning whispers with pastel delight,
As roosters laugh at the softening night.
Clouds scramble, like kids on the run,
While palm trees sway, joining the fun.

A rainbow of colors bursts at the seams,
Like dreams spilling over in bright morning beams.
The sky is a canvas, splashed with good cheer,
While sleepy monkeys scramble, appearing near.

Chasing Light in Paradise

Flitting butterflies in funny pursuit,
Chasing sunbeams like they're fruit.
Each flicker a giggle, spiraling high,
Tickled by tickles in the vibrant sky.

In this realm where shadows play,
Laughter dances, come what may.
Daydreams shimmer on the ocean's crest,
It's a fun fair, where glow worms jest!

The Warmth of Dappled Sunlight

Sunbeams dance on leaves so green,
A disco party, quite unseen.
Lizards groove, they take the floor,
And squirrels join to ask for more.

Coconut drinks give quite a laugh,
When palm fronds wave, it's all a gaffe.
Monkeys swing with cheeky flair,
While bright sun rays tease the air.

A Journey Through Illuminated Landscapes

On trails where shadows play and peek,
Bumblebees buzz, oh what a squeak!
The flowers grin, so bold and bright,
Their colors clash in pure delight.

Bananas wiggle, quite a show,
As parakeets squawk, 'Let's go, let's go!'
Each twist and turn, a new surprise,
As sunlight paints the world in rise.

Crystal Waters and Golden Reflections

A pond that winks with golden cheer,
Fish wear sunglasses, oh so dear!
Ripples laugh, they twist and twirl,
While dragonflies make quite a whirl.

With each splash, the frogs partake,
In synchronized jumps for goodness' sake!
The sun's warm kiss on water's face,
Makes even snails pick up the pace.

Afternoon Glow in the Jungle

Vines hang low, a swinging spree,
As spiders spin their webs with glee.
The sun drips through the leafy maze,
While parrots gossip in a daze.

Bamboo sticks hum a serenade,
While monkeys crack jokes that never fade.
In the jungle, laughter reigns,
And sunshine sparkles like champagne.

Aurora of Island Mists

In the morning haze we wake,
Parrots squawk, and coffee's fake.
Misty hugs bring laughter rare,
Where's my sock? Oh, it's out there!

Sandy toes and coconut drinks,
Crabs dance wild, with silly winks.
Clouds drift low, like sleepy bees,
Making shade for noisy seas.

Sunlit Laughter Beneath Banyan Trees

Beneath the shade where monkeys play,
A leaf drops down—what a ballet!
Laughter ripples, breezes tease,
Sunlight tickles through the leaves.

Banyan branches, twisty high,
Swinging kids, the birds all fly.
Bright-eyed friends with goofy grins,
Who knew fun could cause such spins?

Glistening Brilliance on Summer Nights

When the stars begin to twinkle,
Sea turtles waltz, and crickets sprinkle.
Lanterns sway with giggles loud,
As shadows dance, oh, we feel proud!

The moon's a balloon up in the sky,
Casting light where jellyfish fly.
Sandy raccoons, oh, what a sight,
Under glowing beams, we shout with delight!

Capturing Ephemeral Glories

With each sunset, we pose and grin,
Snapshot moments where fun begins.
Salty breezes mess our hair,
While crabs do jazz, we dance with flair!

Kite strings flutter, like pure delight,
Chasing shadows, we've taken flight.
In every giggle, we find the key,
To hold the dusk as it sets us free.

The Glow of Nature's Palette

Colors splash like paint from a can,
Bright greens and yellows dance on land.
A parrot's squawk, a monkey's grin,
Nature's clowns, let the show begin!

Sun-kissed faces wear a golden hue,
Palm trees wave, saying, "Hey there, you!"
As laughter rings and flips like a kite,
We find joy in a playful light.

Shimmering Tropics at Eventide

As day fades into a gleaming jest,
Cocktails clink; we're at our best.
Sunsets tangle in long shadows spry,
While fireflies twinkle as they flirt and fly.

A crab does the cha-cha on the shore,
While sea turtles slow dance, asking for more.
The sky blushes with mischief and cheer,
Where the night hums softly, "It's party time, dear!"

Dance of the Light and Leaves

Leafy grooves sway like a funky band,
Sunbeams twist, oh, ain't it grand?
Coconuts wink from their lofty perch,
While island tunes make the palm fronds lurch.

Laughter erupts from a passing breeze,
As crickets chirp, with delicate ease.
Twinkling stars join the merry beat,
Echoing joy as they tap their feet!

A Tapestry of Vivid Illumination

At dawn's first light, the world starts to grin,
Crayons spilled on the horizon's skin.
Lizards lounge on sun-warmed rocks,
Wearing shades like, "Wow, what a box!"

The afternoon bounces, a playful tease,
Sipping sweet tea with a wink from the trees.
And as the sun sets with a wink of its eye,
It whispers, "Tomorrow, we'll paint the sky!"

Dancing Shadows of Dawn

As roosters crow and stretch their wings,
A sleepy sun to waking brings.
Shadows twirl in morning's grace,
While monkeys laugh in playful chase.

Coconut squirrels join the show,
With cheeky grins and hearts aglow.
They sneak a snack, play hide and seek,
While the sun peeks out, so bright, so sleek.

Golden Hues

The sky is splashed with mango gold,
As daytime stories all unfold.
Parrots squawk, they hear the news,
About the snacks, the jokes, the blues.

A painter's brush has lost its mind,
Colorful chaos, so unconfined.
The sun, a jester, plays its part,
Tickling the clouds, a work of art.

Whispering Palms

Palms gossip softly in the breeze,
Sharing tales of sunburned knees.
They wave their fronds, a silly dance,
While crabs do the cha-cha by chance.

Breezes tickle, they sing along,
To a lively, breezy, silly song.
A starfish grins, a conch shell snores,
Sea turtles just roll on the shores.

Luminous Horizons in Paradise

The horizon winks, oh what a tease,
As fish wear shades, they float with ease.
A seagull drops its sandwich, oh dear!
While tourists laugh, with waves of cheer.

Sunset's magic is quite absurd,
An artist's canvas, a confused bird.
The moon just rolls its eyes in flight,
And giggles softly at the night.

Sunlit Serenades of the Tropics

Bach's breakfast buffet makes a splash,
As fruits drop down in a vibrant dash.
With every bite, a giggle peeks,
As laughter dances through the beaks.

Karaoke crabs belt out a tune,
While dancers twirl beneath the moon.
A chorus of joy, a radiant sight,
As tropic hearts sway with delight.

Radiance Through Canopy Green

Beneath the leaves, it plays hide and seek,
A sunbeam tickles, oh! What a cheek.
Chasing shadows on the forest floor,
I trip on roots, then laugh, 'Just one more!'

Lizards lounge on branches, striking a pose,
In fashion so bright, they steal the show.
Butterflies giggle, while flowers sway,
Nature's disco ball, come out and play!

Kaleidoscope of Sunbeams

Splashes of light dance like a clown,
On flowers and cheeks, they turn us brown.
Illuminated coffee cups, oh so sweet,
Every sip's a laugh, can't stay in my seat!

Optical illusions, drinks with a twist,
Who knew sun-warmed mangoes could taste like bliss?
Jokes in the breeze, they whisper and sneak,
As I sip the sun from the edge of my cheek!

Embracing the Warmth of Daylight

Here I am, a penguin in the sand,
Catching rays like I just joined a band.
My towel's a stage, my sunscreen's the beat,
Doing the worm, oh, life is a treat!

Seagulls squawk in harmony, showing their flair,
As I throw them snacks with a total lack of care.
Sun-kissed adventures, oh what a delight,
Letting waves tickle toes, feels just right!

Twilight's Embrace on Coral Shores

As the sun dips down, the sky's having fun,
Colors swirl around, nature's own run.
I slip on flip-flops, my dance moves are bold,
But watch out for crabs—they are humorously controlled!

Candles flicker in the breeze with a tease,
Dinner's a buffet of laughter and ease.
Fireflies join the party, a spark in each flight,
Twilight's grip on the beach feels just right!

A Symphony of Sun and Sea

The sun's a clown, with rays so bright,
It tickles waves, they dance in delight.
Seagulls laugh, they swoop and dive,
In this shining circus, we thrive!

A coconut fell, oh what a sight!
It rolled like a ball, caught in sunlight.
The beach ball burst, it squeaked in jest,
As we tumbled down, amid this fest!

Glimmers Between Leaves

In the jungle's laugh, the leaves do sway,
Sunbeams play hide and seek, hooray!
Lizards wink, with glimmers so sly,
While monkeys swing by, oh my, oh my!

The shadows poke fun, they twist and bend,
As sunlight's giggles around us blend.
A parrot squawks, 'What a sunny show!'
And all of us chuckle, enjoying the glow!

Amber Reflections at Dusk

When day winks goodbye with a golden grin,
Frogs croak their tunes, let the night begin.
Fireflies twirl like tiny stars,
They giggle and shimmer, from near to far.

A crab in the sand starts a dance of glee,
While the sunset paints clouds with jelly and tea.
We're all quite silly as dusk draws near,
Echoes of laughter, all shed a cheer!

Waves of Light Upon the Shore

Surfboards bob like playful pups,
While the waves of joy spill from our cups.
Splashing and laughing, we leap with glee,
Serenading the sun, oh can't you see?

Bikini tops fly, like kites on the run,
As the ketchup bottle spills, oh what fun!
With shimmering tides, and giggles galore,
We ride on the light, what a beachy score!

Golden Hour on the Isle

Sun sets like a giant toast,
Melting down, we all just coast.
Laughter bubbles, all around,
As shadows dance upon the ground.

Coconuts wear glasses too,
As sunbeams play peekaboo.
Beach umbrellas, hats askew,
We're here for fun, just me and you.

Sandy feet and beach ball flies,
With every swing, we touch the skies.
Seagulls squawk in happy tunes,
While crabs wear tiny hats like spoons.

When twilight whispers goodnight cheers,
We chase the fireflies, no more fears.
With glow sticks waving, all aglow,
Tomorrow's sun will steal the show.

Nature's Light Through Rainforest Canopies

In the jungle, light takes flight,
As monkeys swing, it's quite a sight.
Leaves whisper secrets, green and bright,
While frogs recite their songs at night.

A parrot dressed in hues so wild,
Calls out for snacks, a hungry child.
Laughter echoes through thick vines,
As we dodge bugs like tiny mines.

Sunbeams poke through leafy seams,
Illuminating our silly dreams.
Sloths dangle, judging our race,
While turtles grin at our quick pace.

Glowing vines twirl like they're alive,
We dance with joy, feel the vibe.
Nature's light, with humor tight,
Turns all our stumbles into flight.

Tides of Luminescence on Seagrass

As waves laugh, they kiss the shore,
Tiny fishes dart and score.
Shells whisper tales of ocean lore,
We giggle as our seaweed's core.

Bright jellyfish laugh at our toes,
Illuminated, their mood just glows.
Sandcastles rise like silly dreams,
While seagulls laugh at our schemes.

Riding tides, we twist and spin,
Chasing sunbeams for that win.
Crabs wiggle, waving claws in cheer,
While dolphins dive, they draw us near.

As the sun dips low, we sigh,
We'll wave goodbye, but oh my, oh my!
With each tide, more laughs will come,
In this luminous world, we are all so dumb.

Dreamscapes Enveloped in Warm Radiance

In a realm where giggles grow,
Sunshine spills like butter, whoa!
Clouds wear hats that float and sway,
While we dance the choreo of play.

Rainbows drape in silly bows,
As we sing to silly crows.
With cotton candy skies above,
Is this the life we dream of love?

Sunny days bring dreams galore,
Each misstep laughs, we can't ignore.
With every sunset, our spark ignites,
In this realm where all is bright.

As the stars twinkle in the night,
We'll dream together, pure delight.
When morning comes, we'll sail away,
In these dreamscapes, we'll always stay.

Chasing Rainbows After Rain

When clouds decide to take a break,
We leap and splash with every quake.
A prism dances in the sky,
We race to catch it, oh so spry!

With ducks that quack and giggles loud,
We join the wobbly, silly crowd.
Umbrellas turned into cheeky hats,
Pretending we are acrobats!

The puddles mirror our delight,
As we dive into the splashing fight.
Who knew the sun could play so nice?
A rainbow, too—oh, what a slice!

So here we stand, with arms outstretched,
Grabbing colors, hearts enmeshed.
With laughter ringing, we embrace,
Life's a game we can't replace!

Sun-kissed Moments in Paradise

In flip-flops wedged in grains of gold,
We stumble, giggle, never cold.
The sun's a cheeky little sprite,
Who sprinkles warmth, setting us alight!

Parrots squawk with a sense of flair,
As we strike poses, unaware.
With drinks adorned with tiny umbrellas,
We're just a bunch of silly fella's.

Beach balls bounce like our wild dreams,
We chase them with joyful screams.
The sand gets everywhere—we jest!
We're just a mess, but that's our quest!

So let's toast to these goofy times,
With laughter that sounds like chimes.
In sun-kissed shenanigans we trust,
Making memories, laugh, we must!

The Glow of Evening's Breath

As daylight fades with a wink and grin,
The fireflies start their dance within.
With palms outstretched, we shout and cheer,
Watching their glow like magic beer!

The sun slips under with a sigh,
As colors twirl, and we just fly.
We roast marshmallows, laughter ignites,
Our giggles twinkle like starry nights!

A breeze whispers secrets in our ears,
As shadows sway and disappear.
We're just a bunch of merry sprites,
Under the glow of moon's delights!

So here's to dusk and its playful tease,
With silly stories carried in the breeze.
We light up the night, oh what a sight,
Evening's breath is pure delight!

Luminescent Nights Underneath Stars

Beneath the twinkles, we set the scene,
With laughter louder than a marching machine.
Glow sticks wave like a dance parade,
As we attempt moves, oh, what a charade!

The constellations wink and smile,
Encouraging our silly style.
With shadows blending into the dark,
We're stumbling like we're at the park!

In this glow of warmth, we find our place,
With fireflies joining in the race.
We throw our worries to the breeze,
In a night where joy is sure to please!

So let's keep dancing 'neath this flicker,
With hearts so light, our laughter's thicker.
In luminous laughter, we'll spin and twirl,
Underneath these stars, let's laugh and whirl!

Illumined Dreams of Coastal Retreats

Seagulls squawk, sun hats fly,
Beach balls bounce, oh my, oh my!
Sandy toes, ice cream drips,
Waves pretend to give us tips.

Flip-flops dance, a lizard peeks,
Sunburnt noses, rosy cheeks.
Umbrellas tilt in wild delight,
Even crabs are feeling bright.

Sunsets humor, painting skies,
With orange giggles, purple sighs.
We toast with drinks, in hand they sway,
While dolphins play, we shout hooray!

Belly flops and laughter shared,
Tropical fun, we are so dared.
Ice cube castles, melt away,
But joy remains, forever stay.

Celestial Wonders Above the Coral

Fishy friends in colors gleam,
While jellybeans float in a dream.
Starfish wink, oh what a sight,
Underneath the moon's soft light.

Snorkels giggle, splashes loud,
An octopus joins the crowd.
Crabs do cha-chas, quite the tease,
Making waves with utmost ease.

Bubbles rise, tickling the air,
Even seaweed joins the fair.
Sandy crowns made with such flair,
Coral groves, the best affair!

Underwater jokes, what a scene,
With laughing waves, we're all marine.
Sunlit giggles fill the blue,
Dancing fish say, 'Join us too!'

Kisses of Light on Vibrant Blooms

Petals stretch, in colors bright,
Bumbling bees take joyful flight.
Frogs in hats leap with glee,
Dancing in the shade of trees.

A butterfly slips on a shoe,
Sipping nectar, quite the brew.
Sunbeams play peek-a-boo,
As flowers bloom, both old and new.

Roses chuckle at the sun,
Tulips whisper, 'Life's such fun'.
Vines entwine in silly games,
While daisies giggle out loud names.

A garden party, all are invited,
With fruits and laughter, all united.
Nature's cheer, what a delight,
In floral joy, we unite!

Sun-kissed Paths of Serenity

Flip-flop songs on sandy trails,
Where laughter and adventure sail.
Palms clap hands, oh what a show,
Waving to all, come on, let's go!

Cats on surfboards, trying to glide,
With sun hats worn at a crazy side.
Lemonade dreams and coconut pies,
Chasing shadows beneath bright skies.

Pineapple fountains with fizzy cheer,
Dancing cool like they don't fear.
Sunsets giggle, pink and gold,
While we share tales, yet untold.

Crickets chirping, night draws near,
With fireflies as our chandelier.
On these paths, our hearts take flight,
In every wink of the warm sunlight.

A Canvas of Vibrant Skies

The sun wears sunglasses, oh so bright,
   Painting clouds in shades of light.
   Parrots squawk their praises high,
   While seagulls chat and pass by.

Palm trees sway in funny dances,
As if they know the sun's silly glances.
   Bikinis flop, the surfboards glide,
      In this colorful, playful tide.

Flip-flops make a silly sound,
   As we skip on sandy ground.
Sunscreen slips, and laughter spills,
   In this land of beachy thrills.

So grab a drink, a fruity blend,
   This vibrant day will never end.
With laughter bright and spirits free,
   Let's toast to this fun jubilee!

Twilight Symphony at the Beach

As daylight fades, the crabs all scurry,
Under the glow, they hurry, hurry.
The sun dips low, a cheeky grin,
While fishermen try, but never win.

Bonfire crackles, marshmallows toast,
Beachcombers laugh, it's what they boast.
Stars pop out, like fireworks bright,
But seagulls claim them, what a sight!

The moon plays guitar, a silver chord,
While kids chase waves, laughing, adored.
A hermit crab steals a tiny snack,
And everyone shouts, "Hey, bring it back!"

With silly dances and joyful cheers,
We cheer the night, with no fears.
In twilight's glow, we prance about,
Under the stars, we laugh and shout!

Elements of Light and Water

Water glistens like diamonds tossed,
As a dolphin jumps, with laughter embossed.
The sun's like a kid with a paintbrush too,
Splashing colors, a magical view.

Raindrops want to join the fun,
But the ocean waves say, "You're on the run!"
While skimmers zoom and boats spin round,
Messy splashes, joy unbound.

Funny fish make faces, oh dear,
As we splash water, a hearty cheer!
Sunsets whisper, "I'm not done,"
While kids shout, "Cannonball! Let's run!"

Together we dance, in sun's embrace,
With silly moves, we find our place.
In light and water, laughter sings,
A symphony of fun, oh what joy it brings!

Radiant Hearts in Tropical Paradises

In the land of bright and sunny glee,
Where the flowers giggle, and so do we.
The sun smiles wide, a golden face,
As we run around in this happy place.

Coconuts bob like friendly pals,
While bananas dance, with fruity calls.
Lizards lounge, in hats too small,
Chasing shadows, they have a ball.

Umbrellas flicker, like pop-up shops,
While juice drips down, from creamy tops.
As sunset paints the sky with flair,
We giggle and twirl, without a care.

Together we bounce, under the sun,
In this paradise, oh, so much fun!
With radiant hearts and laughter loud,
We celebrate life, and feel so proud!

Warm Embrace of Daylight Dreams

Sunshine tickles toes on sandy shores,
While giggles dance on waves and roars.
Palm trees sway, doing the cha-cha,
As crabs in tuxedos join the fiesta.

Bright-eyed birds don their party hats,
While lazy frogs sport sun-kissed spats.
A coconut drops, like a birthday cake,
And the beach bum shimmies—a real mistake!

The sun is a spotlight, quite the show,
Casting shadows that wiggle, just so.
Laughter echoes as flip-flops fly,
Under a radiant smile from the sky.

With a wink, the sun bids night adieu,
As stars pop out like confetti, too.
A melted sorbet in a cone that jigs,
Daylight ends with the silliest of gigs.

Flickering Fireflies Under Canopy

Twinkling bugs wear their nightly best,
Dancing 'round like they're on a quest.
Whispers from the trees start to roam,
While frogs are crooning, 'Take me home!'

Laughter bounces through leafy halls,
While critters in costume play hopscotch and squalls.
Fireflies play tag in the velvety dark,
While a raccoon loudly steals the park.

Moths flutter by, with no sense of style,
Wearing old sweaters that might just beguile.
Flappers of nature with their own delight,
Mingling together in a fantastical flight.

Bursts of light, like birthday cheer,
Flash in the night, bringing us near.
A sparkling jig beneath the moon's beam,
In a world that feels like a child's dream.

Infusion of Radiant Mornings

The waking sun bursts through the blinds,
Stirring sleepy heads and playful minds.
Coffee brews in a boisterous way,
While toast sings out, 'Let's start the day!'

Birds play charades on the window ledge,
Chirping and flapping, a promise, a pledge.
Silly squirrels play leapfrog with trees,
While giggling grasshoppers join with ease.

The sky's a canvas, drizzled in gold,
With masterpieces crafted, wild and bold.
Pancakes on plates are stacking in style,
With syrup rivers that run for a mile.

A sunbeam slips in with a wink and a tease,
Tickling cheeks with warm, gentle breeze.
As the day unfolds its cheerful dance,
Life's but a laugh, if you take the chance.

Serene Light Over Coral Reefs

Coral castles beneath the blue,
Where fish wear shades and giggle, too.
Starfish lounge with a tropical flair,
While turtles play tag without a care.

The seaweed wiggles in rhythmic beats,
As mermaids giggle with their jellyfish seats.
Crabs in bow ties shuffle on sand,
Dancing together, a wacky band.

Underwater sunbeams paint a scene,
Where clams give high-fives, looking quite keen.
Anemones flutter like party balloons,
While octopuses juggle under the moons.

With shimmering scales, they prance and swirl,
A dance of bubbles, a cheeky twirl.
In this playful kingdom, all feels right,
As the ocean sparkles with laughter and light.

Radiance Through the Palms

Sunshine dances on the leaves,
As if the trees just want to tease.
A coconut drops with a loud thud,
To the rhythm of a playful flood.

Monkeys swing, they laugh and play,
Swinging high, they steal our spray.
While piña coladas call our name,
Even seagulls join the game.

Sunscreen's smeared, a messy plight,
In this radiant, joyous light.
The beach ball's loud, it flies away,
Chasing it is half the day.

Flip-flops squeak, they're like a tune,
Dancing barefoot under the moon.
With laughter shared, we feel so bright,
In this glow that feels just right.

Luminous Horizons at Dusk

The sky wears orange like a crown,
As sun slips down, it won't back down.
Seagulls squawk, they call for fish,
While we dream up our next grand wish.

A sandcastle falls, oh what a sight,
With dinky flags of pure delight.
Kids giggle, their buckets all lean,
Building tales of sandy cuisine.

The twilight hues bring funky flair,
Even crabs dance without a care.
Sneaking snacks when no one's near,
While ice cream melts, we all just cheer.

Stars peek out, they join the show,
As waves crash softly down below.
With goofy grins and sandy toes,
Dusk rolls in with comic prose.

Warmth Found in Twilight Hues

As shadows stretch across the shore,
We stumble as we search for more.
The bonfire crackles, sparks take flight,
In tangled tales, the fun ignites.

Marshmallows roast, they start to melt,
Funny faces, all else is felt.
With every bite, we laugh and squeak,
It's sticky fun, but oh so chic!

The tide is ticklish on our feet,
Giggles echo, a joyful beat.
With each splash, a ripple spreads,
As silly songs fill up our heads.

The sun dips down, it waves goodbye,
With painted skies, we laugh and sigh.
In twilight's warmth, we find our bliss,
Even the stars can't resist this.

Vibrant Shadows of Island Life

Under the palms, we chase and shout,
With vibrant shadows dancing about.
A parrot squawks a silly tune,
While crabs march to the beat of the moon.

Hammocks sway, they're like a dream,
In this paradise, we plot and scheme.
A beach ball crashes in our path,
Igniting a whirlwind of laughter and wrath.

With every wave, our worries fade,
As we splash in the sun's parade.
The sunburn's real, but who's to fret,
We wear our scars like a sunny set.

In each twirl, the night grows bright,
With goofy grins, we feel just right.
Island life, in colors so bold,
In shadows vibrant, tales unfold.

The Dance of Light and Shadow

Sunshine winks upon the sand,
While shadows prance like a clown.
Lizards leap and do a jig,
As palm fronds sway, they wear a crown.

Frisky rays play hide and seek,
While laughter bubbles in the breeze.
Coconut boys, all polished and sleek,
Whisper secrets with playful tease.

Flickering beams on swaying trees,
Tickle the toes of the unsuspecting.
Even the crabs join in with ease,
In this radiant, jestful blessing.

The sun shines low, like a round, goofy face,
As twilight brings a spark of glee.
In this silly glow, we find our place,
And dance to the rhythm of the sea.

Sunkissed Dreams of Coastal Bliss

Lemonade skies with a goofy grin,
The seagulls strut like they're in a race.
Surfboards wobble, let the fun begin,
As waves crash down in a giggly embrace.

Flip-flops slap that sandy floor,
While sun hats dance in a comical swirl.
We'll gather shells and then explore,
As the tide pulls in a frothy whirl.

Shadows stretch, making funny poses,
While we chase after the tangerine glow.
Every sunset's a canvas that dozes,
Pinks and oranges meld in a swirl like a show.

Joy resides where the sun meets the sea,
With laughter that bubbles just like champagne.
Each silly moment is a treasure key,
Unlocking dreams in the blissful refrain.

Reflections in the Heart of the Tropics

Mirrors of water, splashy and bright,
Where fish play poker, deal under the sun.
Palm fronds giggle, avoiding the light,
While crabs in tuxedos try to run.

Ducks wear sunglasses, strutting in style,
While the sun plays tag with the waves.
Turtles look on with a cheeky smile,
As they float around in their lazy caves.

The horizon blushes in giddy delight,
With each dip of the sun, a clownish flair.
As night creeps in, we toast to the sight,
Of reflections dancing in the sea's cool air.

Chasing stars through the chuckling tides,
We make wishes as the moonlight imprints.
In the heart of this magic, joy abides,
Held tightly in laughter without hints.

Dawn's Tender Touch on Earth

Morning yawns with a sly little grin,
As roosters crow in mismatched socks.
The sun peeks shyly, ready to begin,
While sleepy heads do their flippity flops.

Bright rays tickle the sleepy blooms,
As laughter bubbles from the trees.
With all the giggles that morning consumes,
Nature dances in its own sweet tease.

A gentle breeze whispers cheeky jokes,
While butterflies wear their finest attire.
Fragrant flowers, like playful folks,
Join the dawn as it raises the fire.

So let the sun's touch light up the day,
With warmth that wraps like a cozy bed.
In this funny realm where shadows play,
Each dawn's embrace paints joy ahead.

Gleaming Reflections on Sandy Shores

The sun slipped in, a golden grin,
Seagulls dancing, doing a spin.
Flip-flops squeak on sandy trails,
Crabs wave hello, revealing their tails.

Beach balls bounce, a cheerful sight,
Children laugh in morning light.
Umbrellas shade the snoozing folks,
While sunburnt dads crack dad jokes.

Tanned tourists flaunt their beach attire,
While slippery fish leap and aspire.
Sandcastles stand with royal flair,
As seagulls plot to steal their share.

Footprints fade as tides come play,
Chasing crabs who scurry away.
In this sun-kissed, vibrant scene,
Life feels like a funny routine.

A Symphony in Sunbeams

Sunbeams sneaking through the trees,
Tickling frogs who laugh with ease.
A parrot squawks a silly tune,
While lizards rock under the moon.

On the beach, a sun hat flies,
Caught by a gust, it waves goodbye.
The surf hums a bubbly rhyme,
As crabs dance in perfect time.

Palm trees sway with great delight,
They shimmy left, and then to the right.
A coconut drops, kerplunk! Oh dear,
But look out! Here comes the beachside beer!

Sun-kissed laughter fills the air,
As sun tanners forget their cares.
In this vibrant, gleaming place,
Laughter echoes, a silly embrace.

Cascades of Color at Daybreak

Morning spills with colors bright,
Pinks and oranges, a pure delight.
A rooster crows, he's quite the star,
While sleepy dogs nap, near and far.

The waves clap hands with glee and foam,
As fishermen toss nets to roam.
Turtles peep with their sleepy heads,
While gecko bands play on their beds.

A catfish wiggles in a puddle,
While dolphins jump, causing a huddle.
They wear sunglasses, oh what style!
"Catch me if you can!" they say with a smile.

As day blooms bright, the fun won't cease,
In this wacky world, there's no release.
With giggles, splashes, and joyous sounds,
We dance beneath the skies unbound.

Whispering Sunrays on Still Waters

Sunrays giggle as they cascade,
Kissing waters, a playful trade.
Frogs in their lilypad boats, float,
While ducks debate who's wearing a coat.

Ripples laugh with a gentle sway,
As fish tease friends to come and play.
"Look at me!" a tiny bug shouts,
In this sunlit dance, there are no doubts.

The dragonflies twirl, a dance so sweet,
As turtles chill on logs for a seat.
Splashing water sends a ripple of cheer,
"Where's the lemonade?" someone calls near.

In the sun's embrace, spirits soar,
With whispers of light, who could ask for more?
Each beam a joke, a wink, a sigh,
In this quirky paradise, we fly.

Enchantment of Light in Bloom

Sunshine spills like honey, oh what a sight,
Flowers nodding proudly, caught in delight.
Bees buzzing gossip of pollen-filled pies,
While butterflies frolic under cerulean skies.

Lemonade sun pops with flavors so bright,
While grasshoppers dance, having a wild night.
Petals play tag with frolicsome breeze,
Nature's own jesters, aiming to please.

Rainbow-colored shadows skipping around,
Awkwardly tripping on soft, grassy ground.
Laughter erupts from the trees overhead,
As monkeys exchange their own silly threads.

Each ray's a comedian, bright and bizarre,
With jokes that would tickle, from near and afar.
In this vibrant circus, oh how we bloom,
Living the punchline beneath nature's room.

Harmonies of Light and Color

Listen! The vibrant hues begin to chime,
Every shade a note, in this rhythm of time.
Clouds fluff like marshmallows, giggling with cheer,
While rainbows become melodies, sweetly sincere.

Golden rays waltz with firefly spins,
While the sun takes a bow, and the moon grins.
Lemon-leaf laughter and coconut croons,
As nightfall paints jokes with the light of the moons.

Squirrels in shades, bright coats they show,
Just trying to keep up with the dazzling glow.
With tufts of joy flying, they tumble and tease,
Creating a riot of laughter in trees.

Colors collide like they're in a big brawl,
With polka-dots dancing and stripes having a ball.
The scene's a circus, so lively and spry,
Filled with giggles and whispers that float through the sky.

The Celestial Dance Overhead

Stars in a line, making their quirky cheer,
Whispering secrets that only we hear.
The moon in pajamas, yawning so wide,
As planets perform with a cosmic slide.

Planets do cartwheels, twirling with glee,
While comets shout jokes, oh can't you see?
The sunlight bursts in with a dramatic flair,
While shadows throw shapes in the fresh evening air.

Clouds dressed in costumes of fluffy delight,
Twirl and float, gaining height, what a sight!
Starlit mishaps, a giggle-filled show,
As nighttime revelers steal the soft glow.

Each twinkle's a wink, a playful retort,
Drawing laughter from dusk till the last report.
In this vast ballroom, where wonder takes flight,
We can't help but chuckle at the dance of the night.

Seeds of Light in Soaked Earth

Rain drops are chuckling, bursting with glee,
Kissing the soil like old friends, you see.
Mushrooms pop up with hats all askew,
In a party of colors, just waiting for you.

Mud splashes laughter, it's stuck on your shoe,
While flowers unearth jokes that embrace the dew.
Rooted in antics, the grass whispers tales,
As rainbows break out without any fails.

Squirrels dig burrows that giggle in time,
Sprouting bright dreams in the mud's slippery rhyme.
Each seed a comedian, sprouting with style,
While worms do their dance and the raindrops beguile.

This puddled playground, a whimsical spree,
Where life and laughter are wild and free.
So come, let's frolic where sunshine will spark,
In the flooded fields, we won't miss our mark!

The Artistry of Nature's Glow

In a jungle where colors collide,
Monkeys hold paintbrushes wide,
They splash the sky with laughter and glee,
While parrots critique, sipping iced tea.

The flowers burst forth in a riotous dance,
Bees join the fun, given half a chance,
Sunlight giggles, peeking through leaves,
While iguanas sport their sun-kissed sleeves.

Even the clouds are soft and absurd,
Floating by like a big, fluffy bird,
They tickle the sunbeam's cheeky grin,
In this art show, we all want to win!

With every brushstroke, the day fades away,
The night rolls in with a cabaret,
Fireflies twinkle, they start the show,
In this gallery where wild things glow.

Paintbrush of the Setting Sun

As the sun dips low with a wink and a jest,
It paints the horizon in a polka-dot vest,
Rays of tangerine dance proper and spry,
While clouds play tag in the warm, golden sky.

Coconuts giggle, providing the blend,
While ocean waves clap, it's a fun, silly trend,
Crabs shuffle sideways, joining the fun,
In this masterpiece made by day's setting sun.

The boats bob along, like they're in a ballet,
Their sails flapping wildly, come what may,
While fishermen chuckle, casting their nets,
In a vivid canvas where no one forgets.

It's an art show of joy, with no time to pout,
With laughter and colors all swirling about,
So grab your paintbrush, come join the spree,
Where each vibrant stroke sets our spirits free.

Luminous Echoes of Ocean Breezes

Breezes whisper secrets from far-off lands,
Ticklish and wild, they play in the sands,
Waves giggle softly, like children at play,
As they tickle the rocks, then dash away.

The horizon's a canvas, stretched wide and bright,
With dolphins dancing, all laughing in flight,
Shells tell their stories, each one a delight,
As seagulls join in, taking turns at the mic.

Even the starfish have jokes up their sleeves,
Wiggling and jiggling, oh how one believes!
They dream of the shore, a whimsical thrill,
In a realm where the light gives you a chill.

And when night creeps in, with its glittering hue,
The moon joins the party, it's a lively crew,
With echoes of laughter that shimmer and glide,
In the breeze of the ocean, our joy can't hide.

Glowing Shores of Remembrance

On shores where the sand is as soft as a joke,
Laughter bounces back with every light poke,
The waves play tag with our toes in the sun,
While crabs scuttle by, their antics are fun.

The sunsets collapse like a joyful parade,
Colors explode, a delightful charade,
Children leap high, chasing shadows that dance,
While parents just chuckle, lost in a trance.

With footprints left trailing, stories unfold,
Each silly mishap, a memory gold,
The sea might forget, but we will not sway,
For laughter and love are the games that we play.

As night wraps its arms around us, we find,
These glowing shores linger sweet in our mind,
So let's fill our hearts with this lovely exchange,
Where joy is the journey, and never grows strange.

Mosaics of Color in Island Bliss

Bright umbrellas pop in the sun,
While tourists trip, oh what fun!
Sandy toes and coconut drinks,
Who knew sunburns could cause such winks?

Parrots squawking, fashion so loud,
A rainbow of colors, they make us proud!
Flip-flops flying in the breeze,
As if they're dancing with perfect ease!

With every splash, laughter echoes wide,
Even crabs join in for a tide ride!
Though the seaweed may tangle our feet,
We just laugh, oh this is sweet!

In this paradise, mischief does bloom,
As we chase sunsets, forgetting our gloom!
With sun-kissed smiles and silly hats,
Life feels grand, like playful acrobats!

Nature's Canvas of Dappled Light.

Sunshine filters through leafy greens,
A hot dog sizzles, bursting our seams!
We're swinging from branches, feeling so free,
Until a bee says, 'Hey, that's my tree!'

The shadows play tag, oh what a game,
Each step is a stumble, quite the acclaim!
Lizards laugh as they dart and scamper,
While we chuckle at nature's grand tamper!

Coconut palms waving like hands that clap,
As we do the twist, forgetting the map!
Nature's vibrant colors swirl and sway,
With giggles echoing, bright as the day!

In this light so playful, we feel quite spry,
Even the butterflies can't help but fly!
Every moment a canvas, rich and bright,
Painting our laughter in pure delight!

Golden Glimmers on Ocean Waves

Flip-flops flinging, with each little splash,
A seagull dive-bombs, we all make a dash!
Chasing the waves, what a silly parade,
Our laughter's the tune—better than any serenade!

Sandcastles rise, then promptly fall down,
A toddler's laugh, wearing seashells as crown!
Sunsets draping, golden and bold,
While I can't decide if I'm hot or cold!

The ocean gives kisses, but bites like a tease,
As we flail in the foam, feeling the breeze!
But who cares for order in this salty spree,
When mermaids might giggle, swimming with glee?

So we roll in the sand, and we dance in the sun,
Generating chaos? Oh yes, that's the fun!
With sun-kissed skin and laughter galore,
Life out here feels like an endless encore!

Sunlit Dances in Canopy Depths

Bamboo shoots sway, making music divine,
While monkeys take selfies, feeling just fine!
Cocoa beans chuckle, sweet secrets to share,
As picnic ants march, creating a fair!

Squirrels do ballet, oh what a sight,
Twirling and twisting, from morning till night!
Mangoes hang low, daring a bite,
But dodging those pits? A slippery plight!

Sunlight sneaks through, like a playful thief,
As laughter erupts, pure and brief!
Nature's confetti, brighter each day,
With friends in the forest, we giggle and play!

Oh, the canopy whispers, secrets found,
With spice and aroma all swirling around!
In this vibrant theater, we let out a cheer,
Every sunlit dance makes joy crystal clear!

Veils of Light in Verdant Hues

Green leaves giggle in the breeze,
Sunbeams sneak through with such ease.
Lizards dance, all decked in gold,
They brag about the warmth, so bold.

Coconuts juggling like they care,
Bananas swing without a pair.
A parrot cracks a silly joke,
While palm trees sway and poke a poke.

Shadows Play on Golden Sand

Footprints chase the waves around,
While crabs tap-dance to the sound.
Kites dive low, they tease and zoom,
Sandy toes cause giggles to bloom.

Tanned folks lie like shriveled fruit,
Seagulls hover, quite astute.
They squawk, 'Hey, you're looking baked!'
While everyone laughs, all smiles are raked.

Days Imbued with Tropical Charm

In flip-flops, we strut with glee,
Chasing shadows like a spree.
Turtles waddle with a wink,
As butterflies sip orange drink.

Pineapples wear their hats askew,
While mangoes sing a song or two.
Every moment's a playful tease,
Under those glorious, swaying trees.

Echoes of Sunlight on Water's Skin

Splashing in waves, what a delight,
Fish giggle as they take flight.
A dolphin shows off a cool flip,
While seaweed sways, an emerald whip.

The sun throws jewels on the sea,
Mermaids laugh, 'Hey, come swim with me!'
Waves whisper secrets from afar,
As sun-kissed folks twirl, like a star.

Flares of Color in the Breeze

Sunshine dances on the grass,
While my hat flies past like a fast-moving class.
Birds chirp in a silly tune,
Chasing shadows under the afternoon moon.

Palm trees sway, doing a jig,
With coconuts rolling like they're on a big gig.
The breeze sneezes through vibrant blooms,
While I laugh with a friend who perfumes the rooms.

Children giggle as they chase a kite,
It flops and flutters, a comical sight.
Laughter bubbles like a fizzling soda,
In this carnival dressed in grand flora.

Soak it all in, embrace the swirl,
For life's too short to spin in a whirl.
With colors ablaze, the world is alive,
In this circus of light, we gladly dive!

Echoes of Sunshine on Forgotten Shores

On shores where shadows play and tease,
The sun bounces like it's trying to please.
    Seashells giggle, whispering tales,
      As I trip over sandcastles and fail.

Waves crash and splatter with frothy glee,
I dodge them all, but they find me, whee!
The beach umbrellas dance, oh what a sight,
Like they're practicing for a joyful flight.

Seagulls swoop down with a comedic squawk,
    Stealing my sandwich—oh, what a shock!
    With each bite gone, I can't help but grin,
      This mirthful day, I began to win.

So here's to the tides and the sun's warm rays,
    Life's playful moments, oh how it sways.
At the edge of the world where laughter flows,
    Under the sparkle where funny life grows!

The Pulse of Nature's Luminescence

In the jungle, the colors start to prance,
A parrot struts as if in a dance.
Lemurs leap with a flair for the fun,
While I nearly trip over a tree root, oh run!

The sun peeks through in a playful stream,
Casting shadows that twist and gleam.
A monkey laughs, flipping high in the air,
While I try to capture it, I'm caught in a snare.

Bouncing flowers wave with such delight,
Like little clowns put on a show, what a sight!
Fireflies murmur their own little jokes,
While I giggle and leap like a band of folks.

Nature shares a chuckle, bright and bold,
In every glimmer of green and gold.
So come join the fun, let your spirit ignite,
In this jungle of joy, where all is just right!

Captured Essence of a Summer Day

In a hammock that sways, I drift and snooze,
While ants plan their road trip, wearing tiny shoes.
The sun spills laughter on my sun-kissed skin,
As ice cream drips, oh, where to begin?

Children splash, making fountains of cheer,
Launching their giggles like rockets, oh dear!
With my lemonade, I take a bold sip,
As it spills down my shirt, what a fabulous trip!

Clouds play hide and seek with the sun's bright face,
While my dog finds a puddle, jumps in with grace.
Squirrels chatter, sharing their grand buffet,
In this hilarious feast that happens all day.

Summer's a stage, all whimsical and grand,
With moments that slip right through our hands.
So let's dance with the joy, let it sway,
In this captured magic of a summer day!

www.ingramcontent.com/pod-product-compliance
Lightning Source LLC
Chambersburg PA
CBHW072223070526
44585CB00015B/1466